12/12

Sea Anemones

Meryl Magby

PowerKiDS press.

New York

For my friends at Beachwood Elementary School

Published in 2013 by The Rosen Publishing Group, Inc.
29 East 21st Street, New York, NY 10010

First Edition

Editor: Amelie von Zumbusch
Book Design: Greg Tucker

Photo Credits: Cover, pp. 4, 5, 6–7, 8, 9 (bottom), 10, 14–15, 21 Shutterstock.com; p. 9 (top) Christopher and Sally Gable/ Dorling Kindersley/Getty Images; p. 11 Tobias Bernhard/Oxford Scientific/Getty Images; pp. 12–13 Paul Kay/Oxford Scientific/ Getty Images; p. 16 Norbert Wu/Science Faction Jewels/Getty Images; p. 17 Jeffrey L. Rotman/Peter Arnold/Getty Images; pp. 18–19 David Wrobel/Visuals Unlimited/Getty Images; p. 20 Andrew J. Martinez/Photo Researchers/Getty Images; p. 22 Doug Allan/ Photographer's Choice/Getty Images.

Library of Congress Cataloging-in-Publication Data

Magby, Meryl.
 Sea anemones / by Meryl Magby. — 1st ed.
    p. cm. — (Under the sea)
 Includes index.
 ISBN 978-1-4488-7401-9 (library binding) — ISBN 978-1-4488-7480-4 (pbk.) —
ISBN 978-1-4488-7554-2 (6-pack)
 1. Sea anemones—Juvenile literature. I. Title.
 QL377.C7M34 2013
 593.6—dc23
                                    2011051476

Manufactured in China

CPSIA Compliance Information: Batch #WKTS12PK: For Further Information contact Rosen Publishing, New York, New York at 1-800-237-9932

Contents

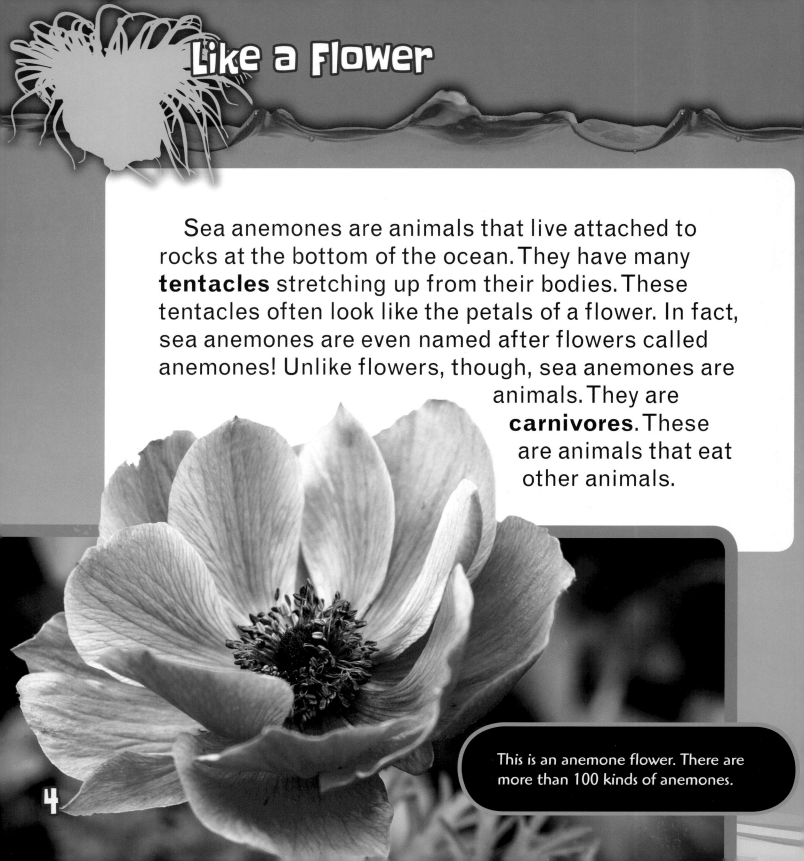

Like a Flower

Sea anemones are animals that live attached to rocks at the bottom of the ocean. They have many **tentacles** stretching up from their bodies. These tentacles often look like the petals of a flower. In fact, sea anemones are even named after flowers called anemones! Unlike flowers, though, sea anemones are animals. They are **carnivores**. These are animals that eat other animals.

This is an anemone flower. There are more than 100 kinds of anemones.

4

Sea anemones are related to jellyfish and coral. Scientists think that the earliest sea anemones and corals **evolved** over 550 million years ago. Today, there are more than 1,000 species, or kinds, of sea anemones living in Earth's oceans.

5

Tropical Water Homes

There are species of sea anemones living in every ocean on Earth! However, most species of sea anemones live in **tropical** waters. Sea anemones can be found at almost every depth of water. Many anemones live in shallow water along the coast. Others live at the bottom of the deep open ocean.

Sea anemones generally stay in one place for their whole lives. Some dig themselves into the soft, muddy seafloor. Most attach themselves to rocks or coral reefs on the ocean's floor. Coral reefs are ridges made of the hard remains of corals. They are home to many animals.

These are called magnificent anemones. They live in the warm waters of the Indian Ocean and the Pacific Ocean.

Soft, Colorful Bodies

Sea anemones have soft, tube-shaped bodies. They attach themselves to rocks or coral with a foot called a pedal disk. A sea anemone's mouth is an opening at the flat top of its body. The mouth leads to a simple gut, where food is **digested**. Many tentacles stretch out around the anemone's mouth.

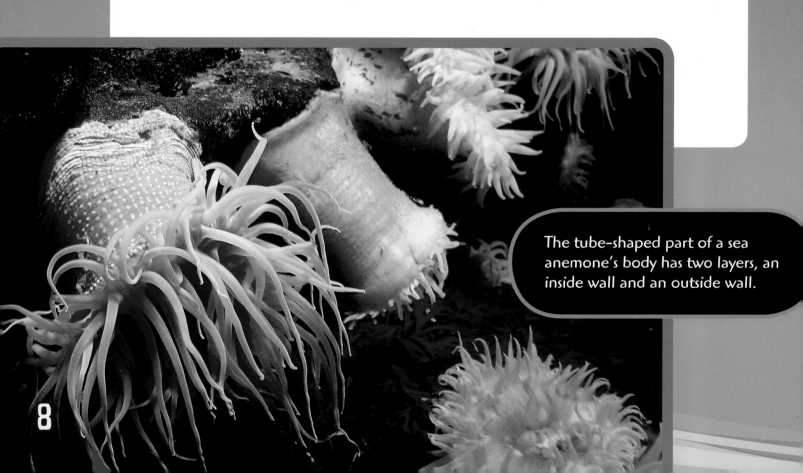

The tube-shaped part of a sea anemone's body has two layers, an inside wall and an outside wall.

An anemone's tentacles can be long, short, wide, or thin.

Sea anemones may be many colors, sizes, and shapes. Common colors include red, blue, orange, white, green, and pink. Some anemones are as small as .5 inch (1.3 cm) wide. Other anemones stretch more than 6 feet (2 m) across!

Stinging Tentacles

Sea anemones have thousands of special stinger cells in their tentacles, as do their relatives jellyfish. These stinger cells help anemones catch food and keep safe from **predators**.

When an animal touches an anemone's tentacles, it sets off some of the stinger cells there. Then, a small thread shoots out of each of

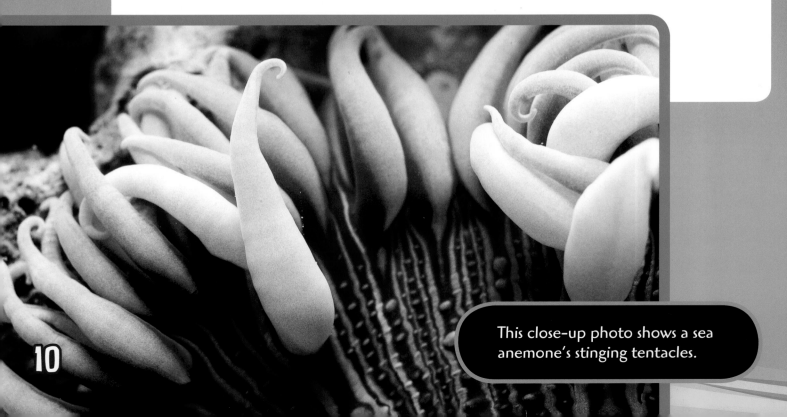

This close-up photo shows a sea anemone's stinging tentacles.

Hell's fire anemones, such as this one, are one of the few anemones that have a sting that hurts people.

those stinger cells and into the animal's body. The thread carries a poisonous substance called a **neurotoxin**. The neurotoxin often **paralyzes** the animal, or keeps it from moving. Sea anemones can even hurt other anemones with their stings. However, most sea anemones do not hurt humans.

Sea Anemone Facts

1. Sea slugs that eat sea anemones often take the anemones' stinger cells and wear them on their own bodies. This lets the slugs keep themselves safe from predators.

2. Most sea anemones do not hurt people. However, there are a few kinds people should stay away from. One is the stinging anemone. This dangerous animal looks like an underwater fir tree!

3. Sea anemones have very long life spans. They can live for between 60 and 80 years!

4. Pom-pom anemones are a kind of anemone that lives in the deep ocean. Scientists have seen these puffy anemones rolling around on the ocean floor.

5 Some anemones, such as the giant green anemone, have tiny things called algae living inside their bodies. The algae make extra food for the anemones.

6 Sometimes sea anemones catch rides on the backs of hermit crabs.

7 Apple anemones are sometimes called swimming anemones. When something bothers these anemones, they let go of their rocks and slowly swim away. Then, they curl up in tight balls!

8 The dahlia anemone covers its body with pieces of shells and sand. It does this to blend in with the things around it and hide from predators.

9 Many sea anemones live in the intertidal zone. This is an area of shallow coastal water that dries out during low tide. Sea anemones living there fold themselves up during low tide to keep their bodies wet.

Anemones in Groups

Some sea anemones live alone. Others live in large groups, called **colonies**. Some sea anemones do not mind living very close to other anemones. Others use their stinger cells to keep other anemones away.

Anemones can move around very slowly using muscles in their pedal disks. Sometimes sea anemones move to places where they can find more food.

Sea anemones often have special partnerships with other ocean animals. These animals include small fish and crustaceans. The sea anemone and its partner animal help each other. The anemone keeps the animal safe from predators, while the animal shares its food and keeps the anemone clean.

Clown fish live among anemones' tentacles. Their bodies are covered with a soft thing called mucus that keeps the anemones' stinger cells from hurting them.

All sea anemones are carnivores. Small species of anemones eat tiny animals called plankton that float in the water. Larger anemone species catch bigger animals, such as bivalves, snails, crustaceans, and small fish.

This strawberry anemone is eating a kind of seaweed called kelp. These anemones eat mainly fish, sea worms, and other animals.

This northern red anemone is eating a starfish. These anemones are also called dahlia anemones. They eat mainly fish and crustaceans.

Anemones catch their food with their tentacles. When small animals come close, they use their tentacles to grab the **prey**. The special stinging cells on their tentacles keep their prey from getting away. Then, the tentacles move the food to the anemone's mouth. Anemones only eat the soft parts of their prey's bodies. They spit out hard parts like shells and bones.

Different species of sea anemones have different ways of reproducing, or making more anemones. Some anemones are not male or female. They can reproduce by splitting into two anemones. When this happens, the new anemone is an exact copy of the first one.

Other species of anemones reproduce with eggs and **sperm**. Some anemones make both eggs and sperm inside their bodies. Others may be only female and make eggs or only male and make sperm. In both cases, the sperm **fertilizes** the egg and a **larva** is formed. Then, the larva grows into a young anemone on the seafloor.

Unlike most sea anemones, brooding anemones spend their first few months attached to their mothers. After about three months, they crawl off and start life on their own.

What Eats Anemones?

Sea anemones do not have many animal predators. This is because the neurotoxins in their stinging cells hurt many animals. However, some species of sea slugs, crabs, sea stars, and fish eat sea anemones. The anemones' stings do not hurt them!

Several kinds of nudibranchs, including the one seen here, eat sea anemones.

Raccoon butterfly fish feed on several kinds of sea anemones.

Sea slugs, also called nudibranchs, like to eat the anemones' tentacles and soft bodies. Butterfly fish are a kind of fish that lives in coral reefs. They tear off sea anemones' tentacles as a snack. Crabs easily rip up anemones' bodies with their hard, sharp claws. Sea stars, also called starfish, use special juices in their stomachs to break down anemones' bodies.

Keeping Anemones Safe

Right now, most sea anemones are not in danger of dying out. However, ocean pollution and overfishing can hurt sea anemones and the coral reefs on which many of them live. If people do not take care of coral reefs, sea anemones and all of the animals that live there may be in danger.

It is important not to dump oil, garbage, or poisons into the ocean. People can help sea anemones and other ocean animals by keeping the oceans clean!

Glossary

carnivores (KAHR-neh-vorz) Animals that eat only other animals.

colonies (KAH-luh-neez) Groups that live together.

digested (dy-JES-ted) Broken down so that the body can use it.

evolved (ih-VOLVD) Changed over many years.

fertilizes (FUR-tuh-lyz-ez) Puts male cells inside a female cell to make young.

larva (LAHR-vuh) An animal in an early period of life.

neurotoxin (nur-oh-TOK-sen) A poisonous thing that attacks the nerves.

paralyzes (PER-uh-lyz-ez) Takes away feeling or movement.

predators (PREH-duh-terz) Animals that kill other animals for food.

prey (PRAY) An animal that is hunted by another animal for food.

sperm (SPERM) A special male cell that, with a female egg, can make young.

tentacles (TEN-tih-kulz) Long, thin growths on animals that are used to touch, hold, or move.

tropical (TRAH-puh-kul) Having to do with the warm parts of Earth that are near the equator.

Index

Websites

Due to the changing nature of Internet links, PowerKids Press has developed an online list of websites related to the subject of this book. This site is updated regularly. Please use this link to access the list: www.powerkidslinks.com/uts/anem/